BIG WORDS
for little hearts

Written by
Susan M. Fuller

Illustrated by
Jo Rooks

Author's Dedication

To the loves of my life,

Josh, who always loved me unconditionally and supported my dreams,
and Sage, who makes me a proud Mama and continues to inspire me daily.

Also, so much gratitude to family and friends,
as we all know it takes a village to live life fully.

Author's Reflections of Gratitude

To all the Sanderson Academy students and staff, thank you for believing.

To the team at Miriam Laundry Publishing, here is to going after your dreams.

To Jo Rooks, for bringing my vision to life with your art.

I am truly humbled.

Copyright ©2022 Susan M. Fuller
Illustrations by Jo Rooks

Photograph of Sue Fuller by Diane Garland
Photograph of Jo Rooks (self photo)

Published by Miriam Laundry Publishing Company
miriamlaundry.com

All rights reserved. This book or any portion thereof may not be reproduced or used in any manner whatsoever without the express written permission from the author except for the use of brief quotations in a book review.

HC ISBN 978-1-990107-87-0
PB ISBN 978-1-990107-64-1
e-Book ISBN 978-1-990107-65-8

FIRST EDITION

Author's Message to Parents & Teachers

I believe in my heart that the younger a child learns words with such big meanings, the more they will be shaped into amazing human beings.

I hope this book helps you teach these big, meaningful words to children—use one word and practice it all week or use a different word a day for seven days. This book is meant to be used over and over again.

Author's Message to the Reader

Each and everyone of us has one mind that has many, many thoughts, one set of lungs to take deep breaths, and one body to move. We can use our mind, lungs, and body to help us through our day. To remember how you can use your mind, lungs, and body, think of these three M's:

mantra
A Mantra is a collection of a few words put together so that they are easy to remember and can be repeated over and over to ourselves throughout the day.

moment
A Moment allows us to find the importance of our breath. We can pause and take some deep breaths in and out through our nose and mouth.

movement
A Movement keeps our minds and bodies healthy and happy. We can stretch, hold a pose, and breathe.

In this book there are seven important words that we will focus on. These words are Welcoming, Gratitude, Patience, Perseverance, Kindness, Caring, and Integrity.

Let's use the power of Mantras, Moments, and Movements (the three M's) to help bring together the meaning of each word.

welcoming

Welcoming means being kind and friendly to your friends, parents and family, teachers, and even people you do not know. You can be welcoming by waving and smiling.

I hug my loved ones.

I wave to my classmates.

I smile at the bus driver and my teachers.

Fun Facts about Smiling

- ♥ Smiling boosts your immune system
- ♥ It is easier to smile than frown
- ♥ It takes 5 to 53 muscles to smile
- ♥ Babies are born with the ability to smile
- ♥ Smiling relieves stress by releasing endorphins

(endorphins are the "feel-good" chemicals in our body)

mantra

I will smile at everyone.

moment

Belly Breathing

Sit with your legs criss-crossed, or lie flat on your back. Start by putting one hand on your heart and the other hand on your belly. Take a deep breath in through your nose and feel your hand rise on your belly. Now let your breath all the way out. Do this two more times. Listen to your breathing. Feel your body relax.

You may wish to use a bell, chime, or a singing bowl. Listen to the lovely sound.

- ♥ Automatically slows the heart rate and helps us to become relaxed and calm
- ♥ Supports the life skill of relaxation
- ♥ Increases awareness of the breath and its effect on the body

In the beginning, demonstrate how to calmly ring the chosen sound. As your child(ren) becomes good at this breathing technique, allow them the chance to quietly and carefully ring the sound.

breathe in   breathe out

movement

Easy Pose

- Sit cross-legged on the floor
- Stretch your spine nice and tall
- Roll your shoulders forward and back
- Gently stretch your neck side to side and forward and back
- Remember to be gentle with your body

Hug Pose

- Give yourself a hug
- Wrap your arms around yourself and squeeze
- Be welcoming to yourself
- Take a deep breath in and let it all the way out

Pretzel Twist Pose

- Reach one hand to your opposite knee
- Put your other hand behind you on the floor
- Twist to look behind you and hold for three breaths in and out
- Come back to facing forward
- Repeat on the other side of your body

gratitude

Gratitude means thinking about the good in your life and being thankful for all the things you have.

When the sun wakes me up, I am grateful for a new day.

I am grateful for healthy food.

I am grateful for my beating heart which pumps blood around my body.

Gratefulness helps kids have more self-control, generosity, self-worth, happiness, and be more optimistic throughout the day.

 I will remember to be thankful.

moment
Heart Breath

Start by placing your finger on the little heart at the center of the big heart. Take a deep breath in while tracing the arrow. Pause at the next little heart and hold for a count of one, two, three. Continue tracing the next arrow with your finger and let your breath out. Repeat this three more times.

A 2019 study published in *The Journal of Happiness Studies* found that gratitude is linked to happiness in children by age 5. This means that instilling gratitude in our younger kids could help them grow up to be happier adults.

movement

Start on either your left or right leg. Do all three poses in sequential order on that leg. Holding each pose for three breaths.

Then switch to your other leg and do all three poses on that leg. Have FUN!

Warrior 1

- Reach your fingertips to the sky
- Lift through your heart
- Bend your front knee over your ankle
- Keep your spine long and hips facing forward
- Straighten your back leg, and firmly ground your back foot

Warrior 2

- Stretch your arms out to your sides
- Gaze at your front hand
- Relax your shoulders
- Bend your front knee over your ankle
- Straighten your back leg, and firmly ground your back foot
- Point your hips to the side

Warrior 3

- Slightly bend your knee to help balance.
- Stretch your arms forward so they sit next to your ears
- Straighten your back leg. As the pose gets easier, work to level your back leg with your spine
- Square your hips with the floor
- In the beginning you may need to help your balance by holding onto something or someone, and that is okay

patience

Patience means being able to wait calmly without complaining.

I wait for everyone to come to the table before I start eating.

I wait my turn in class.

I wait in line for ice cream.

mantra I will wait my turn and not get upset.

moment
Take Five Breath

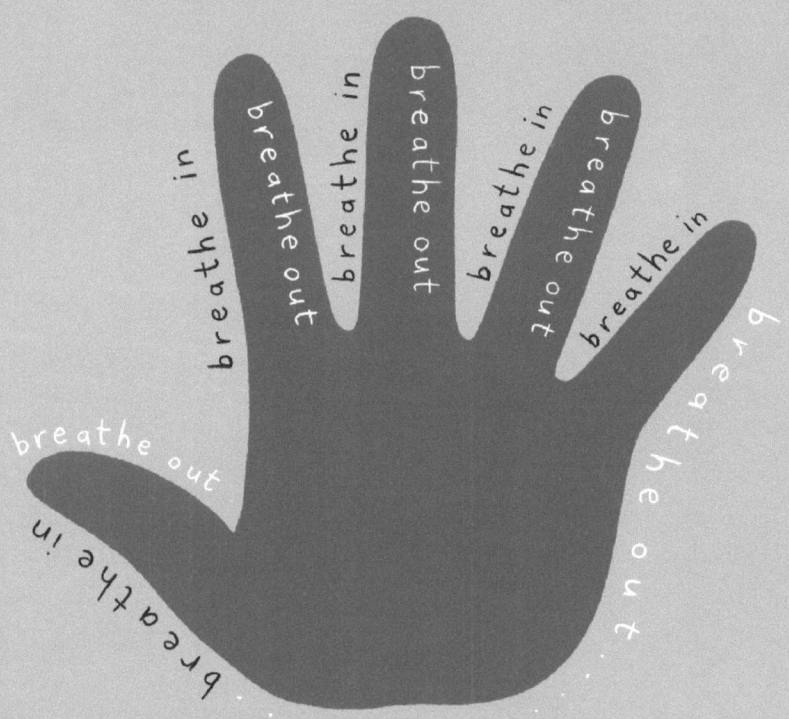

- Put your hand up like you are giving someone a high five
- Use your pointer finger on your other hand
- Slide up each finger slowly and breathe in
- Slide down the other side and let your breath out

You can use a bell, chime, or singing bowl if you want some nice sound to focus on.

Research has shown that listening to the ringing of a bell (or other sound) until the sound fades, starts to create patience. Ask the child to raise or place their hand on their heart when they no longer hear the sound.

Patience is essential to daily life and might be key to a happy one.

movement

The next poses are called Standing Poses. They all include balancing, which is a complex skill that involves the brain, muscles, and parts of the inner ear. Balancing exercises help build better posture and improve coordination, skills that are valuable to the young ones and as we continue to grow older!

Mountain Pose

- Stand tall, with your feet planted firmly on the floor
- Stretch your spine nice and long with your arms by your side
- Take a few deep breaths in and out

Tree Pose

- Bring the heel of one foot up above the ankle of your other foot
- As your balance improves, you can slide this foot up your calf
- At shoulder height, bring your arms out like branches of a tree to help you balance
- Take a few breaths in and out, then switch and do the other leg

Eagle Pose

- Extend your arms out in front of you with your palms facing each other
- Rotate your arms so the back of your hands are together. Move one hand over the other and clasp your hands together. Bring them towards your chest and under your chin
- Focus on your balance as you wrap one leg around the other. Balance on one foot
- Take a couple of deep breaths in and out, then switch and wrap your other leg

perseverance

Perseverance means to keep trying something, even if it is difficult and challenging.

I am trying to learn how to zip my coat and how to tie my shoelaces.

Here are five ways to encourage perseverance in children:

1. Appreciate them for who they are.
2. Focus on their strengths (flex those struggle muscles).
3. Start small and build.
4. Set reasonable expectations.
5. Show them how to plan ahead.

Teaching your child about perseverance will set them up for a lifetime of success.

I am learning how to write my name, even if it takes a lot of tries.

mantra

I can, and I will, learn something new.

moment
Square Breath

→ breathe in for 4 seconds →

hold for 4 seconds

hold for 4 seconds

← breathe out for 4 seconds ←

Breath in.
Hold for a count of one…two…three…four.
Breath out.

Breath in.
Hold for a count of one…two…three…four.
Breath out.

movement

Super Hero Pose

The first pose in this series lets the child(ren) create their own pose!

Here is a chance to get their creative minds going. They will use the answers to the questions below to make their own Super Hero Pose:

- What do you know about Super Heroes?
- Are they strong? Who do they help?
- Do they wear a costume?
- What kind of super powers do you have?
- Create your own yoga pose for your Super Hero!!
- Challenge yourself. YOU got this!

- This is your chance to create your own yoga pose
- Stand tall
- You are STRONG
- You HELP people
- You are KIND
- You are BRAVE
- Hold this pose and breathe in and out three times

Bow Pose

- Lie on your stomach
- With your arms outstretched behind you, grab your ankles and raise your legs
- Keeping your knees hip-width apart, balance on your stomach
- Relax and take a few breaths in and out

Plank Pose

- Lie on your stomach
- Lift your body off the floor by balancing on your toes and having strong arms, hands flat on the floor
- Keep your back as straight as possible
- Keep your neck straight and relaxed

Kindness means being friendly, caring, and nice to everyone.

What does kindness mean to you?

- ♥ Sharing
- ♥ Inviting others to join in playing a game
- ♥ Giving compliments

What act of kindness could you do today?

Kindness is a movement. One small act of kindness can cause a ripple effect that can impact your family, school or community.

Has anyone been kind to you? How did it make you feel? Did you share a similar kindness with someone else? How did that person feel?

I tell my friends I like their cool shirts and neat shoes.

I hold the door for others.

mantra
I will treat everyone as my friend.

moment
Dandelion Breath

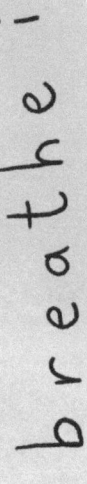

breathe out
breathe in

Imagine that you are holding a beautiful, fluffy dandelion.

Take in a deep belly breath. Hold for a moment, and then gently breathe out through your mouth as you imagine you are blowing all those dandelion seeds everywhere! Think about sending out kindness wishes to everyone. Repeat a few more times.

movement

These poses are called Heart Openers. While these poses do stretch your heart muscle, they also strengthen your back, shoulders and abdomen. These poses also reduce anxiety and stress and boost feelings of self-confidence.

Bridge Pose

- Lie on your back with your arms by your sides
- Bend your knees to the ceiling, and keep your feet firmly on the ground
- Lift your hips and pelvis to the sky, but keep your head, neck, and shoulders on the floor
- Hold the pose and take a few breaths in and out

Camel Pose

- Kneel on the floor
- Reach back to grab your feet and lift your chest to the sky
- Hold this pose and take a few breaths in and out
- If this is really hard, you can rest your hands on your bum instead of grabbing your feet

Cobra Pose

- Lie down on your belly
- Place your hands just in front of you, shoulder width apart
- Lift your head and shoulders off the floor and look straight ahead
- Hold this pose and take a deep breath in
- Breathe out and hiss like a snake
- Repeat a few times

Caring means I like you and want the best for you.

How can we raise caring children?

- ♥ Model positive action
- ♥ Show how to be a good listener
- ♥ Express concern
- ♥ Show appreciation
- ♥ Treat your child with respect
- ♥ Coach your child to notice others' facial expressions

Teach them to show care and concern for others. Be kind even when others are not. Help find a way to help others. Setting good examples will be the best way for your child to learn.

I share my toys with others.

I help my friends when they are hurt.

I cheer for my friends.

mantra

I will be a helpful friend to others.

moment
Rainbow Breath

Think about all the beautiful colors of the rainbow. Start at the cloud with the sun in it. Take a deep breath in and, using your finger, trace up the red color to the middle, pause (hold breath) and then slowly let your breath out as you go down the other side of the rainbow towards the raindrops. Do this for each of the colors.

movement

Rag Doll Pose

- Stand with your feet just slightly apart
- Bend your upper body forward at your hips
- Relax your spine and neck
- Take a few breaths in and out

Downward Facing Dog Pose

- Start by getting down on your hands and knees
- Keep your palms flat on the floor with your fingers spread
- Lift your knees away from the floor
- Lift your hips to form an upside down V
- Hold and take a few breaths in and out

Child's Pose

- This can be done from the Downward Dog pose
- Lower your knees back down to the floor
- Sit your bum on your feet, with your arms reaching out in front of you
- Lower your forehead to the floor
- Relax your body
- Breathe in and out a few times

integrity

Integrity means being truthful and honest and doing the right thing, even when no one is watching.

Be a role model.

Know that children are ALWAYS watching.

Let them hear you say please and thank you.

Help children believe in themselves.

Show what courage, honesty, and respect can look like.

Admit when you are wrong.

Teaching your child(ren) Honesty and Integrity at a young age will make the world a better place.

I admitted to taking the last cookie.

I obey the rules.

I made a pinky promise to my friend, and I plan to keep it.

mantra

I will make good choices.

moment

Star Breath

Start at the white dot at the top of the star. Breathe in and breathe out as you continue to follow the star pattern with your finger.

To challenge your breathing, pause (hold) at each point on the star and then continue.

breathe out · breathe in · breathe in · breathe out · breathe out · breathe in · breathe in · breathe out · breathe out · breathe in

movement

Chair Pose

- Stand in Mountain pose, with your feet slightly apart and breathe in
- Breathe out and bend your knees, as if you were about to sit in a chair
- Extend your arms forward, palms facing in
- Hold for a few breaths in and out
- Stand back up into Mountain pose

Star Pose

- Spread your feet wider than hip width
- Stretch your arms out to your side
- Hold and push your feet into the ground
- Breathe in and out a few times
- Challenge yourself by balancing on one foot
- Hold and do one breath in and out
- Try the other foot and breathe in and out

Crescent Moon Pose

- Start in Mountain pose
- Bring your feet just a bit apart
- Breathe in and bring your arms up over your head, palms touching
- Breathe out and curve your ribcage and arms together to one side
- Breathe in and out, and then move back to center position
- Curve in the other direction and breathe in and out

Hearts for You!

Hearts are everywhere!

Everyone deserves to find them.

Images from Ms Sue's heart-shaped rock collection are included throughout this book.

Which heart-shaped rock is your favorite?

She uses them with her students on a daily basis to pause for a moment and share something they are grateful for.

If you stay curious, you too can discover many heart shapes around you!